Levi Washington

Love Isn't

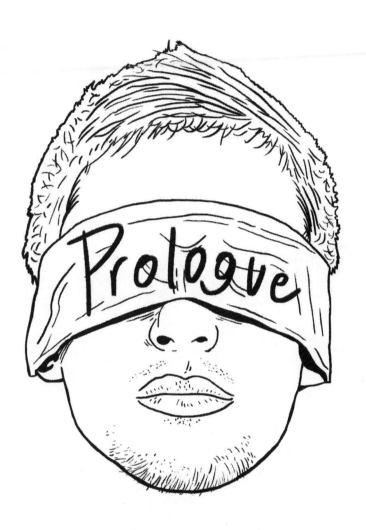

Love isn't

You know what it is
if you know what it isn't
You know what to look for
of you know what you're missing
It all feels the same
if you don't know the difference
It all feels the same
wicked games— *we've been conditioned*

How can we expect to find something we wouldn't even
recognize if we found it?
The search for what love is often begins with
an understanding of what it isn't

A note from the author:

Dear reader,

My hope for these pieces of my heart is that they do not poetically ruminate on cycles of brokenness but that they create space for challenge, hope, and growth. This is not some vain attempt to convince the world that I possess all the answers, but, it is an exploration of the power and freedom that can be found in asking better questions. This book does not follow the choreographed structure of timelines or chapters, as I believe a story of love found and lost, broken and mended, is impossible to capture in a table of contents. It is messy. It is imperfect. It is an ebb and flow, a creation and erosion, a learning and unlearning—it is a dance of life and death between two souls, and my hope is that a few dots will find their connection through the parallels you discover in my story. When we walk alongside one another, in the parallels of our brokenness, we discover the paths of our healing.

Sending love,
Levi

This boy
That girl

There are many sides to every story. The road is paved before it begins; it falls apart before it ends. We find ourselves, and we lose ourselves—over and over again. Maybe the question of it all is: Did we ever truly know ourselves to begin with? *Will we ever?*

debt

Love
I wish we would have known what it was
    before we tried to make it
I wish we would have known what it would cost
    before we tried to break it

From the incomplete blueprints our parents gave us, to the counterfeit definitions society sells us—the idea of love in our lives is too often twisted and battered beyond recognition.

- Based on your experiences, what one *word* would you use to define *love?*
- How would you define this *idea* of love in three to five sentences?
- Has *this definition* of love changed over the years? What did it look like before? What people or events in your life have had the greatest influence, positive or negative, on your definition of love?
- Are you currently living in accordance with your own definition of love, or in response to someone else's actions and definitions?

wandering eyes

we are intrinsically entranced
by the infinite chances that enchant us
by the intimate dances between ques-
tions and answers
behind the innocence of passing glances

"The grass is always greener on the other side of the fence." We have all heard this cliche, and yet, we continue to trespass. Is it desperation? Is it ignorance? Is our vision so impaired by the muddied perspective of our own mess? We must understand that no matter how tempting the opportunity of a blank canvas may look—that canvas, in and of itself, will not make us better painters. Is it not tragic how we have mastered the art of creating the same chaotic mess, over and over, canvas after canvas? Would it not be ridiculous to continue to blame the canvases? When will we see that climbing over fences to chase mirages of greener pastures will never save us from ourselves? We must remember—wherever we go, we are there. We must consider that in the equation of repeating patterns, we are the common denominator—do the math.

It's become a strange familiarity
to seek familiarity in strangers

Every time I look at you, I am looking for someone else. Cinderella is nothing more than a fairytale—you can't fill these glass slippers. I know it. You know it. Yet, we both deny it. Maybe one day it will just "click," right? "Fake it until you make it," right? As long as you continue to remind me of the past, I can see you in my future. Frankenstein is just a story—I can't mix and match all my favorite parts. As long as I am hanging on to what is behind me, I will be unable to take hold of what is right in front of me. If I refuse to let go of either, I will remain torn, divided, and insecure. I will continue living with one foot on either side of the fence named integrity.

I was blinded by the fear that I
would never find
another field of butterflies
inside of another's eyes

No one will ever make us feel the same way that we once felt with someone else. It is impossible to recreate the magic of past experiences, which are always further distorted by nostalgia. Do not waste your life attempting to relive memories and feelings you once had and that you are disproportionately attaching your identity to. They cannot be replicated. As long as you're looking through the lens of the past, the present will never measure up. Be warned; depression and regret wait like silent shadows on your doorstep—salivating, feeding on your thoughts, until they grow powerful enough to swallow you whole.

vagabond

We are strangers at night
dancing down side streets of
cities that don't know us
hoping to find something concrete to hold us
We are ghosts roaming alone beneath streetlights
seeking atonement for words left unspoken
in a life that does not repeat twice

We play in the shadows, we hide who we are, we fear being known, we keep people at a safe distance, and yet our souls crave those very things we are running from: to be seen, to walk unashamed, and to be accepted and loved despite all of the things we want to hide. In my life, intimacy was the drug I used to feel close to that— even just for a moment—validated, important, powerful, wanted, loved, open, and vulnerable. Only to face the inevitable, insidious, all-too-familiar emptiness, begin to mix with the reality of my skin-deep integrity—scratching, clawing, and creeping in like the morning sunlight through the shades, as yet another taxi pulls up.

I hate that you aren't her
I love that you aren't her

Confession—I knew from the beginning that I was looking for the pieces of you that reminded me of someone else. I hate to admit it, but those were my favourite pieces of you. Maybe someone has looked at me in that way before too— It's not unlikely. It's actually kind of funny in a twisted sort of way to think that it was those very pieces that I clung to when you first betrayed my trust—it was not even you I was hanging on to. It was an idea of you—an idea of us. So maybe it was I who betrayed myself, after all? I knew from the beginning. I wasn't there for you; I was there for me. You filled the space. You numbed the pain. What I've learned since: abusing painkillers often leads to addiction.

My broken peace
Your broken piece
You believe I'll fix you
I believe you'll fix me

Jagged edges perfectly matched like a forbidden jigsaw puzzle. Intensely satisfying symmetry and chemistry while in fleeting moments of alignment, but a serrated double edge at the slightest offset to the equilibrium. "When it's good, it's really good, but when it's bad, it's really bad." Some call it passion, but I have come to know it by it's true name—poison.

The years
the tears
the fears
My dear
who taught you how to love?

We can only give from what we have first received. Therefore, we need to ask, *What does the definition of love we have been given look like?* Because the love we are able to give can only be a reflection of that. Tragically, our definitions of love have far too often become eroded, broken, and abused beyond recognition as a result of our experiences and traumas. If we continue to receive our definition of love from those conditional, broken, and temporary places and people, the love we will be able to give will remain equally conditional, broken, and temporary. This includes the love we are able to give ourselves.

outrunning shadows

Maybe I still mention my ex a little too much
Maybe your touch still hurts a little too much
Your fingernails feel like the tips of those daggers
       pressed against my back again
                Two steps forward—
and I am back again

The barbed blade of betrayal tears deep into our flesh and causes extensive internal damage. Trust becomes nothing more than five meaningless letters that leave a bad taste in our mouths. Trust issues are difficult to heal, especially if we do not diagnose and treat the wound properly. Consider that carrying trust issues into new relationships with people who did not break our trust makes us the common denominator by default. Therefore, healing trust issues is less about trying to learn how to trust others and more about relearning how to trust ourselves. The real problems are that we don't trust our own ability to choose whom to trust—because we were wrong before. And we don't trust our resilience and strength to be okay if someone breaks our trust again. Our ability to trust ourselves is the foundation of our ability to trust others.

internal bleeding

Wounds not yet become scars
will bleed through what has not yet become ours

Wounds left without proper treatment will fester and poison our blood. We can become infected to the point we will have no choice but to amputate entire areas of our bodies to survive. Our hearts and minds are no different. Consider this if you feel like your experiences and relationships seem to continually leave you with less and less access to the love, trust, patience, kindness, and courage of who you once were. It is of paramount importance to properly treat, heal, and rehab our wounds. Do not be too proud to seek professional help and therapy. Would you not see a surgeon if your body required surgery? Don't let your ego make you a hypocrite or keep you from freedom and healing. Remember, even though the scars and memories will remain, scar tissue is stronger than regular tissue.

From distractions to attachments
masking the past gets faster with practice

We often use numbing or stimulating behaviors to avoid discomfort and pain. It's important to recognize that these are natural defense mechanisms, but they will keep us from dealing with reality until eventually, we start to lose sight of it altogether. Maybe we look to narcotics or alcohol, maybe we escape into video games or social media, maybe we bury ourselves in our work, or maybe we jump from relation-ship to relationship. But if we continue to look to external sources for temporary relief from discomfort and pain, rather than deal with the root of the problem, the patterns will not only perpetuate, they will dig themselves deeper.

escape

I guess some things take time
I still enter rooms looking for the exit signs

Be aware: if we are mapping out exit strategy scenarios in the early stages of our relationships, spinning webs of pre-meditated excuses and justifications for it to end in our minds—then we are being dishonest with ourselves by even being there in the first place. This is not just about avoiding hurting other people (empathy is not always the strongest motivator). No, this is about eroding trust with ourselves. As long as our integrity is for sale, our relationships will remain cheap. We will never heal our trust issues with others until we first learn to quit lying to the person we see in the mirror.

If it's not about love
it's about fear
They do not coexist

When our hearts are not in a state of love, only then is fear allowed the space to creep in. The further we move away from love, the more room we give to fear to crawl into bed with our insecurities and our scars. It is only in the absence of light that darkness can take hold. Shadows begin to form into the shapes of our fears, whispering of abandonment, rejection, judgment, and pain. Small voices that, before long, manifest themselves into jealousy, control issues, depression, and anxiety. It is only love that holds the power to silence those voices. The closer we align ourselves with love, the quieter fear becomes as a result. One of the problems is that love or at least what it was meant to be cannot be found in the broken, flawed, conditional definitions written onto us by our relationships with other people—people who carry their own scars, definitions, experiences, and fears. So we must work to unravel those definitions and redefine them for ourselves. Consider that maybe it is not love that is the glue holding our reality and our relationships together—maybe it is fear.

devoured

When it's neither black nor white
wrong nor right
those without sight will fall through
the cracks it's teeth leave behind
Beware the beast that hides beside
blurred boundary lines

A world without boundaries inevitably descends into chaos. What is to keep us on the straight and narrow path if not our values and boundaries? It is written, "All things are permissible, but not all things are beneficial." So where do we draw the line? Who is to calibrate our moral compasses? Should we leave Pandora's box to the whims of our conditioned, indoctrinated, trauma-ridden, selfish, individual biases and desires? If we stand for nothing, we fall for anything. There is not much good to be seen on the horizon for a society, let alone a relationship, hell-bent on removing all boundaries and consequences under the guise of "empowerment" and "freedom."

love is enough

They say *love is blind*
I say *we are blind to love*
Why else can we go our whole lives
and never seem to find *enough?*

What more do we desire than to be fully known and
unashamed?
To be imperfect and damaged, but still worthy of uncondi-
tional love?
To know our life has purpose?
To be remembered?
Everything else the world tries to sell us is nothing
but smoke and mirrors, counterfeits we are
seeking to fulfill these very things—to fulfill our
broken, poorly translated definitions of love.

unquenchable

Even this
will not be enough
to fill the cup of what you've been missing
Understand the difference
between *love*
and *addiction*

No amount of numbing or stimulation from temporary external sources will be enough to satisfy the voids within our souls. In fact, the gratification and temporary relief we find externally will only become fuel to the fire—forcing us to constantly increase the dosage. It is imperative that we become aware of our vices and patterns and what triggers them. Ask yourself, where do you turn to quench your thirst when you feel empty or overwhelmed?

mirror mirror

I loved you most in the moments
you looked like *someone else*
but now I see
I wasn't talking about you
I was talking about *myself*

Our relationships are reflections of us. Judgment, disappointment, guilt, shame, unforgiveness, comparison— the presence of such toxicities when dealing with others can often indicate a projection of the way we see ourselves. It is helpful to approach others by first considering that maybe what we are feeling toward them may not even be about them! A poor relationship with what we see in the mirror will inevitably be reflected in the way we are able to see the world outside its frame.

Beneath the surface
she seeks relief for the wounds she nurses
She simply searches
to somehow feel just a little less worthless

Temporary validation from external sources is like a topical treatment for internal issues. Numbing creams and pain killers will not fix what requires surgery. Too often we sell our future for relief and comfort in the present, which only leaves us with a past marked by regret. Nothing is without sacrifice, so try to consider the cost of the long-term debt.

work of art

Beneath guided fingers
the lies still linger—
a painted disguise to hide her figure
compromised
configured
despised
disfigured
tired of running from the fires of hell
tired of replying *"I'm fine"* when
someone tries to help—
tragic is the life lived dying behind
pretty pictures of someone else

Stop trying to paint other people to fit your picture.
Stop painting yourself to fit theirs. Such desperate need
for control and acceptance will only leave us grasping
at straws and impaired from seeing true colors. It
is a tragedy to live our lives as passengers, as empty
shells of people we never knew, hopelessly search-
ing for the love we could never find in ourselves.

when stars align

You lied
beside me in the grass
On our backs
we watched the moon as it danced into silent align-
ment with the sun
Hand in hand beneath the shadow of a solar eclipse
I glanced over at your lips
and wished
that your words and your actions could do the same

If we find ourselves having to ask someone for an alignment between their words and their actions, be very cautious moving forward. Quite often the response or ensuing "change" will be temporary because it lacks the sincerity of their sovereign decision. A truly sustainable change in behavior must ultimately come from within. It is commonly said: "Talk is cheap" or "actions over words," but that does not give words the respect they deserve. Words hold immense power, and we must listen to them closely— more specifically to the intentions behind them. It would be ignorant and naive to simply call it black and white, to say that one is more important than the other, because it is in the space between words and actions that the real answer *lies*—pun intended. That is the space where words and actions meet, intentions die, and integrity is born.

But it was I who came undone
trying to take love from the wrong ones

I spent the majority of my romantic experiences, taking from love. An empty cup seeks to be filled. I covered up my emptiness with Band-Aid relationships. I walked on them like crutches. It was not my heart's intention to use or hurt anyone, but I took what others were willing to give me because it allowed me to feel okay, even if just for a moment. The problem is, from a place of enable-ment—I never learned to walk. I never learned to heal. I blamed the crutches. I was angry. I was insecure. No one was ever enough, but that's only because I was never enough. When we seek love and fulfillment in the wrong places, we will never be satisfied. Whether it be in our romantic relationships, our bodies at the gym, in material success, filling our cup from any external, temporary, and limited source will ultimately become our undoing.

broken records

When apologies keep repeating the same reasons
when does it start to defeat the meaning?

Stop ignoring patterns. Stop lying to yourself. Stop lying to them. Stand for your boundaries. If you do not, it will cost you your integrity. And if you don't have integrity, what do you have to stand on? "Whoever walks in integrity walks securely," *Proverbs 10:9*.

The rejection I couldn't take
was the reflection you couldn't face
The space between remains
We are two sides of the same page

Pride cannot take a loss. Pride cannot own mistakes. Pride ghosts. Pride chases. Pride loves comparison. Pride hates competition. Pride is vengeful. Pride plays the victim. Pride boasts. Pride seeks pity. Pride thirsts for validation. Pride never asks for help. Pride is entitled to help. Pride knows everything. Pride claims ignorance. Pride is self-righteous. Pride points fingers. Pride is judge, jury, and executioner. Pride is beyond reproach. Pride is a tyrant. Pride is a martyr. Pride becomes its own god. Pride comes before a fall.

No one is enough for her
She is not enough for anyone
She is not enough for herself

Instead of choosing people and then chasing them down and begging them to value you, choose your values first. Your value system will chase away the people who don't have the capacity to value you. Understand—the people who come into your life are the variables; your values, your character, and your integrity are not.

He knew he could never lose her
as long as she still had something to prove

It's hard to lose to a loser. Often the most difficult people to walk away from, are the very people we don't even consider to be deserving of us. We believe they should be grateful for everything we've done for them, for a chance to breathe the same air as us, and we need them to acknowledge that, and we can't walk away until they do. We need to prove to them, but more importantly, to our own ego-- that we are better than they are. Pride is a prison disguised as power.

framed

The skeletons in our closets look awfully similar
Maybe I can convince you that you were the killer

If we are too afraid to wrestle with the skeletons inside our closet, if we are too weak to take hold of responsibility, if we cannot lift our eyes to see past our own shame and guilt, if we are wounded and backed into a corner—we will resort to self-preservation. Gaslighting, playing victim, aggression, manipulation—behaviors borne of conditioning and desperation become fair game when we feel like there is no escape, when our very identity is at stake. They say, "All is fair in love and war." And while desperation is not justification, and reasons *why* are not alibis—maybe we need to consider that we are not above those whom we consider sinners. Might we consider that maybe we would become that which we deny under a clear sky when the storm approaches? Might we consider that we all have a price? In the words of Carl Jung, "No *tree, it is said, can grow to heaven unless its roots reach down to hell.*"

If I don't know who I am
I'll have to take your word for it

If you do not learn to weigh and measure your worth by your own scales, you will be weighed and measured by the scales of someone else's opinions and expectations— whether that be your parents, your peers, Hollywood, or social media. Stop putting what is between you and God into someone else's hands. *Define* or be *defined*.

surrender

A serpent and a sailor
tangled beneath waves in the night—
a canvas and a painter
angles, shades, and lines—
they are one and the same; fates intertwinedtheir
deadly embrace, a game of the mind—
It's not in my nature to give up in a fight
but a danger of pride is it's failure to rec-
ognize when red flags turn white

Pride is a blindfold. When we tie it tightly over our eyes, we become unable to see the truth, even if it were to hit us square in the face. Yes, we might feel the pain, but we will not understand why we feel it or where it came from. To survive, pride will lash out in any direction that may feel like a threat, without mercy, empathy, or a second thought. Swinging wildly, we will cause harm to everything and everyone around us and ultimately, to ourselves. Pride does not understand logic or reason; it only knows how to preserve itself at all costs. Our egos hardly think twice about trespassing a weak boundary in order to win, to have needs met, to be validated, to be vindicated. Pride will cry victim, pride will use violence, pride will manipulate, deny, ignore, and all the while justify itself as self-righteous and innocent.

How many times can we untie our soul ties?
"I'm yours, you're mine."
How many times did I fall for that old line?

Do not mistake poison for passion, addiction for loyalty, fear for love. We do not own each other. We do not owe each other. Consider that when we invest deeply into anything, we hope for a return on our investment, naturally so. But when it leaves us empty-handed, save for unmet expectations, unrealized dreams, and unrelenting pain—it's awfully difficult to come to terms with. We will hang onto the ship, refusing to let go, even as it slips beneath the waves. Tragically unaware of the fact we are only a stone's throw from the shore. Is this how it must end? Two people, refusing to let go, sacrificing themselves for some distorted notion of love? Two hearts locked in a deadly game of chicken—whoever gives up first loses? Why do we continue to hang until our lungs fill with salt and water? They abandoned this ship long ago. The line that separates dying a martyr and dying a fool—is thin.

Let's play a love game:
whoever leaves first *loses*

Pride refuses to "lose," to be the "bad guy," the one who "gave up." It waits for an excuse, an alibi, a self-righteous justification to save face and play the martyred victim. Sometimes the chains that keep us prisoner in our toxic relationships are built out of our own ego. We may have had the key in our pocket the whole time—an unimaginably hard pill to swallow, especially when all we have on hand to wash it down with are regret and shame. Consider how someone who is struggling with a gambling addiction refuses to walk away from the table when the chips are down. The more that gets invested and lost, the harder it becomes to throw in the towel and walk away. Put the shovel down.

calling all angels

Let me tell you what I don't think—
that love was ever intended to be a broken thing
But go ahead
keep telling your friends that *you're okay* over drinks
I guess even angels can't see their own broken wings

If you suffer physical trauma but refuse to seek professional medical attention and rehab, it is unlikely that you will heal properly. Do not be deceived—time alone does not heal. With time, the pain may subside, or maybe you can learn to cope and adapt to avoiding use of the injured area. But sooner or later, when a situation requires you to put pressure on it, you are going to be in a world of trouble. You will likely have to re-break the brokenness all over again in order to reset it and recover from it. The rehab process must not be ignored. It is not an overnight fix; it requires responsibility, knowledge, commitment, sacrifice, blood, sweat, and tears. Understand that if this is tried, tested, and true for a physical injury, it would be naive to believe that the injuries sustained to your heart are any different.

false security

Clipped wings and cages
sharing passwords and locations—
I get it, trust has been broken
but it's only to control that we are holding
We will only be left with unspoken regrets
the day the cage door is left open

We have no real control over another person's free will in our relationship. We cannot seek to tyrannically impose our laws, values, expectations, and insecurities on the behaviors of others. Control does not change the desires of a heart. A wedding ring does not guarantee faithfulness. Our pain does not oblige anyone to avoid causing us more. Our forgiveness does not mean they owe us a debt. We must understand, our actions and our responses are sovereign from what anyone else says or does, and we are only responsible for our own integrity. It does not matter how hard you try to make someone understand how you feel. It does not matter how many ultimatums you give. It does not matter if you share passwords, locations, or check in every hour. These control strategies offer a false sense of security. A person must desire to change their behavior for themselves, not from guilt or appeasement, lest it only be temporary. If you have to repeatedly ask someone to put themselves in your shoes—stop. Put your shoes back on, and walk away. A cage will not change a bird's desire to fly.

I couldn't trust you as far as I could throw you
I'd lose my mind every night I couldn't hold you

Too many relationships are held together by nothing more than the smoke and mirrors of power games and trust issues. Too often it is more about codependency and addiction than it is about love. Too few understand that it is from a lack of self that we find ourselves desperate enough to extort and cling to external sources to give us value and validate our existence.

nothing was the same

All you could taste were her lips
every time you kissed me
All I could think
about was your hand in his
every time you told me you missed me

Why do we choose to remain in places that are causing us agony? Why can't we seem to simply remove our hand from the fire? Why do we let ourselves burn until there is nothing left but an unrecognizable pile of ashes? Is it pride? Is it fear? Because it definitely isn't love. The reality is we will almost always choose to remain in a familiar pain than to step into the fear of the unknown.

erosion

Love tastes different on the lips of innocence
before mouthfuls of bliss erode into sips of bitterness
Woe to the victims of it's insidious sickness
weary, broken, and addicted
Futile is the resistance to its persistent incisions
division after division
There will be nothing left of what it is
until we can admit what it isn't

Love can become so mangled and disfigured by trauma that it is left unrecognizable—maybe even sickening to look at or think about. Many of us are left wondering what it was even supposed to look like in the first place or if it ever existed at all. I will not sit here and lie to you about my own healing; I will not deny the physical response that still slams into my spine at the mere sound of the words, "I love you," as if to somehow become physically impenetrable to emotional vulnerability. Am I so emotionally unavailable? Do I even want to heal from this mechanism that serves as an excuse to avoid pain, shirk responsibility, and seek out validation and sympathy for my brokenness? I mean, I have come a long way already, but I still have to force myself to spit out those three little words through gritted teeth and usually out of politeness rather than from authenticity. Where is the disconnect? Am I beyond repair? I have to regularly remind myself that even though I am not where I want to be, I am not where I used to be. One thing I have come to realize is that the journey to where I am has looked a lot less like figuring out what love is and a lot more like removing what it isn't. Therefore, I feel I must continue in that direction in the name of love, pruning away death and decay in order to continue to plow the space that is the fertile ground necessary for growth and healing.

You said I still feel like *home*
I guess *home* doesn't mean the same thing to everyone

Just because it's comfortable does not mean it is good for you.
Just because you can't imagine your life without
it does not mean it is meant to be in it.

I was as ready to be with you
as I was to be without you

When you don't feel full with them, you keep one foot
out the door. When you feel empty without them, you
keep one foot inside the door. If you have torn apart
in the doorway, it's you who are divided, not them.
No one person has the capacity to fulfill the void in
our hearts that stands solely between us and God.

I'm afraid hearts don't break the same beneath the
pale moonlight
in dark corners where shadows and ghosts of haunted
pasts hide
We fight what lies unseen; we are confined by what
we invite inside
All the while time silently creeps behind
the seamless veils of sleepless minds

I watch the silhouettes of the ceiling fan blades rotate in the dark, around and around—insomnia. Replaying past regrets over and over and over—depression. Fantasizing over scenarios of how the future could have been or should have been—anxiety. Unable to trust the present moment, so I live somewhere else. I have sold my integrity. I have given up my ground. I no longer trust myself. There will be no sleep where there is no peace. There will be no peace without a fight. So fight. Fight to stop compromising. Fight to find yourself again. Fight for your integrity. Fight for today, for yesterday cannot be changed, and tomorrow has enough worries of its own. Fight for your peace, and when you have battled enough of your demons so that they no longer lay in your bed beside you, maybe then you will close your eyes and find rest.

I know I made a mess of it
I tried to keep my actions and my emotions separate
but I was desperate
I wasn't dead yet
but I was left for it

More often than not, we know. Deep down, *we know*. And yet, we stay. The question is *why?* Take some time today to write about an experience from your life where you consciously stayed in a place of toxicity and pain; then ask yourself *why*. I mean *really ask*. And after you come up with an answer—go deeper.

Apologies and reasons *why*
will never repay the sleepless nights

A reason or an apology will never balance the scales. They can't pay back the debt. They can't replace the tears. They can't erase the scars. They can't fix what has been broken. As long as we are hunting our past for validation and vengeance, we will not find salvation and hope for our future.

failure to stop

I am now convinced our brakes are broken
until we are broken by our breaks.

We live reactively. Proactive, we don't know what we have until it's gone. We don't make a change until the divorce or the diagnosis. Rock bottom is the only thing that seems to redirect us, but it does not have to be that way. You do not need to suffer from a third-degree burn to know that fire is hot. It is often a lack of self-aware-ness, a lack of boundaries, a lack of understanding, a lack of knowledge, a lack of teaching that causes us to make choices to place ourselves in situations where we are playing with matches and gasoline. And you know what they say about those who play with fire—

Why are those who love us most
those who always get the worst of us?

It is insidiously easy to let the relationships that are "always there" for us to fall into neglect and decay. Instead of investing ourselves authentically in those we hold dear, we often opt to prioritize polishing our masks to play charades for the temporary gratification and acceptance of strangers. Maybe it's because we are safer and more comfortable walking the path of least resistance, avoiding the vulnerability and intentional work required to build relationships. Maybe it's human nature to take the things we have access and proximity to for granted. Either way, the grass is greener where you water it.

There are never enough reasons
Their reasons are never enough

Poor questions will give us poor answers. When we ask ourselves a question, our minds will automatically reach for the most convenient answer—typically the answer that most efficiently absolves us of responsibility or the answer that further confirms our preconceived biases. We don't always find solutions and freedom in asking, *Why?* So instead, try asking, *What?*

If you ask, WHY *am I never good enough for committed relationships?* your mind might say, *Because I'm unlovable, because I'm ugly, because all men or all women are liars and trash.* These are not helpful answers.

If you start asking WHAT? *q*uestions, those answers will change the game. WHAT *patterns are repeating? WHAT am I saying yes to? WHAT am I not saying no to? WHAT am I expecting from others that I am not giving to myself?* Try it out. I dare you. *Why?* questions will keep you a prisoner and a victim. Yes, they may help you understand what materials your chains are made of, but they will not free you from them. *What?* questions will give you the keys to your freedom. No one else can remove those locks. No one can save you from yourself.

the mist

I miss the old me
I miss the old you
I misunderstood
I misread
I mistook
I misled
I miss alot of things

Do not mistake passion for addiction. The chemical releases of dopamine, serotonin, and oxytocin have the power to turn even the strongest of people into fiends in the name of love. Volatile, abusive, codependent, toxic relationships will fill your veins in one moment only to send you spiraling into withdrawal the next. Before you know it, you can find yourself strung out on "love," willing to sell your entire sense of self-worth for just one more hit. Disclaimer: if you become accustomed to the skyscraper highs and the rock bottom crash-and-burn lows of toxicity within addictive relationships, anything healthy will seem uncomfortable, unnatural, numb, boring, and tasteless. Healing takes time.

It's easier it is to walk away from someone
who can't seem to move on because they need you
than it is to walk away from someone
you can't seem to move on from—
because they don't

We want what we can't have. We don't crave accep-
tance until we feel rejection. We need to prove we
are good enough. The wildest thing is the less deserv-
ing we think they are of us, the more we need to prove
our worth and the harder it is to walk away. Our
ego refuses to accept losing to a loser. Walking away
requires immense strength and humility. We must under-
stand that their rejection does not define our worth.

11:11

I wish I could hate you
I wish I could separate your existence from mine
I wish I could be made new
I wish I could relate to those who insist I'll be fine

Our minds, while in the throes of withdrawal after a break up, will seek out familiar patterns. Muscle memory grasps at anything that it still recognizes amidst the chaos and pain of the unknown. Maybe we suddenly start seeing the type of car they drive everywhere. Their favorite color, their favorite food, their favorite number, that show on Netflix—they seem to be everywhere now that they are nowhere to be found. Maybe we even go out of our way to feed the addiction. (creeping their social media updates or hanging on to their personal items). We must understand that while moving on takes time, time alone is not enough. As long as we continue to feed those thought patterns, they will persist. Our minds can't tell the difference between recalling memories and reliving them.

They are never far from my mind—
memories of late night drives
the smell of your hair mixing sweetly with the
evening summer breeze
the taste of your honeyed chapstick on my lips
the comfortable familiarity of our intertwined fingers
the soothing vibration of the friction between rubber
and pavement beneath us
guided by streetlights
lost in the shuffle of a playlist

I am hanging on to everything. I am hanging on to nothing. I replay the words you left me with until the tapes begin to fade from my mind—and then I reread them, and I rewrite them, and I press play once again. I am condemned to relive my own death a thousand times over every sleepless night I spend sober. Well, maybe "death" is being a little over-dramatic-- I am still alive after all, at least I am breathing. Well, that is until the thought of you steals that breath from me, and my lungs collapse on my stomach again in sick, suffocating silence. I sit alone in this prison cell, staring in disbelief at the screenshotted evidence of your crimes against my humanity. Why am I the one doing time? It's like maybe if I stare long enough, it will disappear like it was all some sort of fever dream, but every time I look, nothing changes. I am hanging on to the expired box of your favorite cereal; it's still in the cupboard. I am hanging on to those hand-written letters; they are still in the bedside drawer. I am hanging on to nothing. I am hanging on to everything.

Time is the one thing they said
it would get better with
maybe that's just because with time,
things tend to get less relevant
like that box in your closet that you
used to keep our letters in
for whenever the good times needed remembering

Time does not heal everything. Time erodes every-
thing to dust—dust that we often sweep under the rug.
Out of sight, out of mind. We can pretend to ignore
it, just so long as no one steps on the rug or looks
too closely; I guess we can no longer allow anyone to
get close enough to enter our home now, can we?

right where you want me

You left your hooks in my skin
It hurts when I pull away
It hurts when you reel me in
The only place that remains without pain
      is the limbo spread thin between you and me

Some nights I sleep next to you—as your forever. Some nights I sleep next to you—as a stranger. This push and pull between you and I, has knocked me off my feet. I don't know who I am or what I stand for anymore. I just want relief from the pain and confusion. While my mind knows better, my heart is convinced you are the antidote to the poison running through my veins. I am strung out on you. Withdrawal from you is withdrawal from the drug. I am possessed, wretched, and alone—desperate for a moment's respite. I am bankrupt—willing to sell my soul for just one more hit. How many times can I forgive and forget all the pain and destruction you cause for one more smile, for one more text good morning, for one more long kiss goodnight?

self-portrait

I painted my skin to fit within the
frame of your picture
I have set aside my religion
I have set fire to the scriptures
I only trust in fiction
I've only had enough liquor, if it's
chased with more liquor
Fear and love are a dangerous mixture

The storms of life are inevitable. The rain will come. And when it does: the paint we used to conceal ourselves to look a certain way or to fit a certain image will be washed away to reveal the true vulnerability of our identity that even we may no longer recognize.

Nostalgia is a *hopeless* romantic

Rose-colored glasses and rearview mirrors do not mix. When a destructive relationship comes to an end, do not lose sight of reality.

ransom

With every step ahead
I find have less to lose
I left myself behind
just to stand next to you

Understand your boundaries. Stop choosing people before choosing your values. Far too often, we lock our sights on someone we see as valuable only to lose ourselves, desperately chasing them down to see the value in us. If we would instead build our home upon our values, there would be no rooms available for the people incapable of valuing us.

She put her head on his chest
but no longer recognized his heartbeat

We aren't the same people we were yesterday—neither are they. We build false realities and limitations around other people, and when they break that image we had created of them, we refuse to accept it. It is important that we create space for other people to show us who they are, not who we think they are, nor who we want them to be. Sometimes it feels like someone can become a stranger overnight, but that's not always the case. Yes, maybe they were wearing a mask, and we fell for the clever disguise, but we also have to consider that maybe we had been choosing to live in a false reality of our own construction, of who we wanted them to be. Building such falsified realities acts like a blindfold to any red flags and numbs our ability to feel, let alone trust, our gut instincts. When we do see the truth, we have a choice to make. The damage is not our fault, but healing is our responsibility.

the world is not enough

If you want someone to give you everything
the world will not be enough for you
If you want to give someone everything
that will be enough for your world

No external source can remedy an internal leak. Far too many relationships are built on the foundation of, *What can they give ME? How do they make ME feel? How do they benefit MY life?* While our needs are important, we must understand that no one is capable of providing enough to fully sustain us—to heal us, to keep us satisfied, happy, or faithful. If fulfillment does not come from within, we will always feel like we are without.

That said, do not ignore the presence of the monster that waits like a wolf in sheep's clothing on the other side of the coin. We can find ourselves giving from a place where we expect others to act in accordance with our expectations and to treat us how we believe we "deserve" to be treated in return. Understand—even generosity can be from an insidiously disingenuous, controlling, manipulative, and insecure place that is seeking leverage from a position of self-righteousness and martyrdom.

Those who only know how to give will ultimately wind up with those who only know how to take—codependent, unfulfilled, resentful, locked in an eternal power struggle. Our relationships reflect who we are. "As water reflects the face, so one's life reflects the heart." Proverbs 27:19.

read between the lies

You tell me you're not in love with him
You tell him I'm still in love with you
I wonder what you tell yourself

It is for lack of integrity that inner
peace will elude us indefinitely

I call
She answers
All that matters is
I still have her

It's about power. It's about control. It's about making sure someone will always be there to stroke my ego or to nurse my wounds. I do not think twice when I venture out in violation of boundaries because my needs are more important, and I know you will always be there when I come back. Fill my cup. Serve me. Enable me. Blame yourself. You are trapped and helpless. Your chains are psychological—you have to stay with me to prove you are *enough for me* to change, to win me, to beat me at my game. You can't leave, or else you will become the villain you have been fighting against your whole life—abandonment. You're never enough for me. You are never enough for yourself. You have been told how much you are worth your whole life. Therefore, as long as I can keep you convinced of your worthlessness, I own you. Are my actions one hundred percent conscious? Maybe not. I cannot understand health because I am starving. I cannot see that consuming everything you are will still not be enough to satisfy my hunger. I drink and I drink and I drink, and still I thirst. Your love cannot fulfill my emptiness, but I remain convinced that it is supposed to.

Maybe I've got to tell myself that it's over
Maybe I've got to give myself the words
you never have the courage for—
when you're sober

Closure cannot be obtained from an external source. Apologies and reasons *why* are hardly more than topical treatments. They may aid in our logical comprehension of a behavior and provide temporary relief, but they cannot cure the disease. Chasing closure is self-deception. In reality, we typically chase excuses to continue to hang on to hope, or because our ego is still trying to win. We need to be acknowledged, we need for them to admit they were wrong, we need them to understand that they were the bad guy—they need to know our pain, and we need a reason that's "good enough" to validate our own. But no reason will ever be "good enough." No excuse will repay the debt, tears, or the sleepless night. No apology will ever make what happened okay. "Closure" is a myth. The hunt for what doesn't exist may feel like it numbs the emptiness with a modicum of purpose, but it's a fruitless endeavour—we are fighting our own shadows. The truth of freedom can only be found within.

do not pull

My white-knuckled pride holds
tight to control the rope
with one side tied around my heart
and the other around my throat

Holding on to control is a recipe for disaster. We must learn to let go of the outcomes; we must learn to let go of our false claims to all the things we believe life owes us. What do we *really* "deserve" after all is said and done anyway? To own our dream house? To go on a vacation every year? To have access to running water? To wake up tomorrow? To take our next breath? Gratitude can only flow freely in the absence of entitlement.

assassin

The knives are so deep in her back
Their red tips extend through her chest
She is walking death to the one
who holds her next

Our past pain often becomes our present poison. Our relationships have not always given us tools; sometimes they have given us weapons. Sometimes these are the tools of survival we inherited from our parents. Sometimes these are the blades of betrayal we had to pull from our own backs. Whatever the case may be, maybe it's time we turn the weapons meant for our destruction into the tools meant for our healing. Somewhere along the line, someone has to decide that enough is enough.

diagnosis

You didn't break my heart—
you bruised my ego
Love can walk away—
it is pride that can't

Pride often disguises itself as love. But love is not desperate. Love is not self-righteous. Love is not vengeful. Love does not thirst for validation. Be reminded, if you know what love isn't and begin the painstaking task of ridding yourself of those counterfeits, you will begin to move closer to what it is.

Closure is internally found,
not externally received

The idea of closure is a funny thing—imagine if our freedom hinged on other people's ability to face their mistakes and take ownership of them? Is our strength limited by the weakness of others? It can't be true, and yet so many of us act like it is. Maybe it's easier to blame. Maybe it's easier to remain broken. Maybe it's easier to chase reasons and excuses. Maybe we refuse to do the work because they haven't done their part of it yet. We lay down and make our home in the "refuse" because we refuse to get our hands dirty to clean up the mess we didn't make.

springtime love

Love feels like snowflakes
falling onto the warm spring earth
pure and beautiful they fall
only to disappear once again
as if they were never there at all

I saw you the other day; I know you saw me too. I don't understand why you pretended like you didn't, why you passed within five feet of me and avoided my eyes like I was some sort of wanted criminal. You are the one bringing someone new to the places that used to be ours, to the places where you know you'd find me. I can't help but wonder if you're trying to recreate some sort of sordid replica of what we had. Maybe it's just all in my head, maybe it's just my ego talking, but I swear—sometimes it really feels like I never even knew you.

You feel
like snow melting between my fingers
like time holding its breath before spring
like the contrast of a warm exhale
against the cold night air
as the words fail to form on my lips
Good bye

Let go of what is not yours to control. Take full respon-
sibility for what is. The line that separates the two will
lead to the wisdom required to change the stars.

erosion

Every time you say it's over
I trust you a little less
Every time I wake up sober
I love you a little less

The sobering reality is that our words become worthless when we are unable to hold our ground with our actions. Rule of thumb: if your feet cannot stand by it, do not allow it to leave your lips. If you are willing to say, "It's over," then be sure you are ready to end it. Idle threats will devalue your integrity. Your words will erode into worthlessness. Your anger will become a joke. Your cries for help will be ignored like the boy who cried wolf. Jesus himself once said, "Let your yes be yes and your no be no."

shovel

Desperation digs its own grave
in the name of *love*

Love is not desperate. Desperation comes from attempting to control what cannot be controlled. Controlling others. Controlling outcomes. Begging. Ultimatums. Threats. 20 unanswered calls. 500-word text messages. Unwelcome visits. Fake social media accounts. In any of these situations, the love is already dead, and we are only digging a deeper grave from which it will never be able to climb. Stop calling it "never giving up." Stop calling it "love." It's not. Love can let go. Love can walk away. Love allows others to move how they choose. Here is the key: you must love yourself more than to allow your worth and identity to become so tied to what is not yours to control that you become dependent and desperate.

evicted

Broken and abused
I have closed room after room
There is no space left to live in
Even a home can become a prison
I pray my bones don't break beneath my covers
or when I fall to the bottom of another
bottle between lies and lovers—
will I ever find my meaning from the mess?
That every time I'm breathing I would die to forget—
will I ever find my freedom from the debts?
That every night my demons come alive to collect—
I sold my soul for closure
I sold my soul: foreclosure
From my heart I have been evicted
There is no space left to live in
those with no home become their own prison
solitary soldiers—soulless and separated
sentenced to seek solace and shelter in strangers

If you haven't built a home within yourself, you will have to begin living within someone or something else.

I've been relearning what it means to be vulnerable
I can't remember how it feels to mean it when I say
                                    I'm in love with you.

I have become calloused. I can't feel anything anymore.
Maybe the blade didn't cut deep enough. Maybe the smell
of my own burning skin didn't repulse me enough. Is it a
cry for attention or a cry for help? If I tell the truth when
they ask, *if they ask*, if I'm "okay," will I be met with care
or pity? I don't know. All I know is that I am embarrassed
of the scars beginning to form on my arm. I need to hide.
I need to stop before anyone notices, but I so desperate-
ly want them too. I want them to love the things I hate
about myself so I don't have to. This road is a dead end.
I can see the signs. Why do I continue to ignore them? I
need to turn around. But I am afraid I can't be redeemed.
I am afraid it's too late for me. I am devoid of innocence.
The colors faded a long time ago. I cannot remember how
joy feels. I'd give anything for a moment of contentment.
Will I ever be enough? Will I ever feel again? I guess there's
only one way to find out, and I have nothing to lose.

best wishes

Do you remember blowing eyelash-
es from the tips of our fingers?
How would you feel to know that
those wishes still linger?

I wish I could climb inside your head. I wish I could dissect your heart. I wish I could understand your thoughts. I wish I could understand how you feel. I wish I could make sense of everything that has happened. I wish I could let it all go. How can such a simple, logical solution be so impossible in practice? I have come to believe that grieving lost love is harder to accept than death—at least with death there is finality. There is no closure here, no resolution, no tactile or foreseeable end to you and me. No, instead, I am condemned to this prison while you go on living, laughing, loving, building the dreams that were once ours somewhere else with someone else. Moulding new memories between your fingers to place them like handfuls of dirt over the casket you buried me alive in. Discarded, after everything we had been through, frozen somewhere between "no matter what" and "never again." I am powerless. I am voiceless. I pound with bloodied fists on the looking glass that separates us in my mind—the words left unsaid, the dreams left unrealized. I am haunted by the "what-ifs" that I can't drown when there's nothing left in my bedside glass. I confess that I have known for a while that, in order to save myself, I must walk away. Have I not had enough? Enough desperation? Enough trying to control outcomes? Enough saving face? Enough victimhood? Enough sleepless nights? Enough—my dreams for you can remain intact with or without me in them. Enough—it's time I dream for myself again. Enough—all I've ever wanted to be.

Change that lasts is based on internal decisions
never external demands or conditions

Boundaries are not meant to be violently forced onto other people's free will—that is a trench. We engage in trench warfare when we attack and erode other people's boundary lines with our expectations. We cannot force people to fall in line with how we think they "should" or "shouldn't" behave. Consider that any behavior changes made from this place will likely be nothing more than temporary compliance—a moment of fragile peace until rebellion and resentment inevitably begin to stir in the shadows again. That is not a relationship; that is a political campaign for power. Build boundaries; stop digging trenches.

broken records

Good and bye—
who knew the two words I never heard
would become the two words I'd
stutter over and over?
I've gone around one too many times
on this damned rollercoaster

It's wild how many times we will close the door on someone who is hurting us only to open it again to them at the first knock. We try to hit them with the door when they leave; we try to slam it loud enough, hoping that a moment of pain or the noise will be enough for them to acknowledge our pain and change accordingly. But at some point we need to stop trying to change people who come through our door, and change the lock on the door instead. Closure-- "close-your" doors to people who only ever trespass into your home to lie, steal, and kill, and then leave you to clean up the mess alone.

amnesia

I've been trying to draw your face with my words
but I can't seem to remember it
I guess that's what it means to go
from everything to irrelevant

You still cross my mind from time to time. More often than I'd like to admit, but less often than before. It's a curious thing, the harder I try to forget you, the more your ghost haunts my mind. I've been learning that freedom is not about forgetting where I've been. Healing is not ignoring the pain. Interestingly, I thought I had escaped my addiction to you, but instead, I simply tied myself to a new vice of my resentment and unforgiveness towards you. I became the victim, and whether that holds some truth or not, I've realized that in either case, you are still at the nucleus of my power. I blocked you. I unblocked you. I blocked you again. I have to stop putting my energy into a place that continues to steal it. I have to remove the drugs from my system, I need to get clean. I have to stop pretending it doesn't hurt, I have to stop hoping you will wonder about how I'm doing, and come crawling back just so I can close the door on your fingers... So that's what I've been doing, and it has been working. I no longer try to forget and regret-- I now choose to accept and to bless.

potter's wheel

You carved your name into the walls of my heart
Sharpened blades, some scars never fade
From what starts to what remains
What was torn apart, will never be the same
Maybe we can call it art
Brushes of blame mix shades of shame to cover
canvases stretched over frames of pain
I am too ashamed to pray
A slave to the things I am too afraid to say
It will only be when I learn to break like clay
that I may return to the potter's wheel

A heart hammered mercilessly by pain and fear becomes jagged and jaded. What is left is a fragmented mess-- sharp to the touch, dangerous to those who get too close. While in a state of survival, we are relatively incapable of having a moldable, open heart. When we perceive anything we do not know as a threat, in an attempt to protect ourselves, learning and growth become impossible. A heart of stone will never become flesh again until it can learn to put it's guard down. This is the vital importance of finding community with those who can create the space for us to learn that it is okay to not be okay. Healing that which is within will not fully reach our skin until we can allow ourselves to be seen by others.

I know it hurts
but maybe it has to

Our brains are hard-wired to protect us from pain and discomfort. This is only overridden by our fear of the unknown. We will choose a familiar pain. Therefore, we must consider that the only way we will ever step off the ledge, is if it becomes more painful to stay on it.

Part of my healing has been praying
that she finds hers too

I didn't know whether I should pray that one day you would have to eat your own words. I didn't want you to starve to death on their emptiness, but I also wanted you to understand my pain. I did not realize that I would find my freedom in forgiving you.

Dear reader,

Write a thank you letter, a letter of gratitude and goodwill, to someone you would much rather curse. What lessons did they leave you with? What painful experiences helped shape the beauty within you today? Bless them, and release them on their journey.

Sending love,
Levi

I tied my self worth to you
You were my leash
until you pulled away and became my noose

When you tie your worth, your identity, and your direction to another person, you turn them from your companion-- into your compass. It will not be long before you have no identity or direction of your own. It is a bad idea to put yourself into such a compromised position where you will be utterly lost without someone else telling you where you are, and *who you are.*

no man's land

Absence is
the desolate space
where the borders blur
between the states of love
and addiction

"Absence makes the heart grow fonder," is what I was told. Absence can turn a functioning user into a withdrawal-fuelled fiend, is what I learned. Distance and absence are some of the most interesting environments to observe our behaviour patterns. We live in a world without breathing room, drowning beneath a constant stream of stimulation and validation, a world where we can't go for more than an hour without a text back, or for ten minutes without checking our social media. I wonder how loud the voices of codependency and addiction will become when we are faced with radio silence.

Stop calling it love
It never was

Anger. Pain. Elation. Hope. Fear. Passion. Attraction. Disgust. Disrespect. Apologies. Distance. Intimacy. Extremes are magnetized to each other by their polarity. The violent push and pull of power between people disguises itself as passion and purpose. If your relationship feels like a roller coaster that you can't seem to get off of, do not ignore the sickness growing in your gut. Do not mistake passion for poison.

I can still hear the music that danced in her eyes
because I'm still singing the blues

That smell, that song, those quirky habits. When our brains create familiar pathways and associations, it takes time for those patterns to fade-- but, time alone does not heal. If we continue to walk down the same worn pathways in our minds, we will not allow nature to take its course and grow over those paths. Unless we begin to choose to take alternate routes, we condemn our-selves to walk the same road forever. Reminder: moving forward is not about forgetting where you've been.

"good-bye"
a cruel oxymoron

Grieve the loss. It's okay. It's necessary.

footprints in the sand

do not be deceived
what you perceive to be true from where you stand
is not seen complete through an eternal lens
best believe- *even the ocean ends*

Stop the car. Have a look in the rearview mirror. Replay the memories, both happy and painful, *"the good, the bad, and the ugly."* How many of these past situations are you still currently stuck in the middle of today? Always remember-- *"this too, shall pass."* You can not change the past nor can you control the outcomes of the future, the only thing you have power over is the presence which ironically is the steering wheel that determines both past and future. You chose to read this page today, you can not unread it, and now you can choose to read the next, or not. Be mindful of the power of the present moment.

Baby, I know you've been burned
but you can blame them for *why* you're hurt
or you can blame them for *what* you've learned
Maybe it's time to measure the distance
between questions dismissed, and lessons discerned

We are always quick to make laundry lists of the things we blame others for that have caused us pain. That dirty laundry piles up quickly, and underneath is a breeding ground for resentment and hate. While this is a natural, and effective, coping or defence mechanism that is simply trying to keep us safe, it does not create space for healing or learning. A victim mentality is a prison. The ability to apply learning and healing to our lives to find our freedom can only be unlocked through the keys of gratitude and forgiveness.

It's easy to blame people for the negative things they have brought to your life. Try blaming them for the good things, the lessons, the strength,

the one

when they see your scars
the stars will not change
like the night sky, they will stretch out
their arms and the hold space
to hear stories of the battles you have faced

If you cannot see me for my past, I can not see you
in my future. I understand I am not for everyone, but
I do not need everyone. What I find most interest-
ing— those who have the courage to peel back the most
layers of themselves, will find they have the most in
common with each other. We find our parallels in our
broken places. Why don't we take our masks off?

infinite

Loving you was like chasing the horizon
Moving on has been like outrunning my shadow

It's not that they broke your heart. It's that they broke your expectations of who you thought they were, of who you thought you were, of where you thought you were going, of where you thought you'd been, and that's why it has left you lost, confused, and betrayed. But you are not broken. You've simply lost your direction because they had become your map, compass, and survival kit-- a position of power they were never supposed to hold over your life.

I don't need your *kind of love*
your *"kind of"* love

Love is betrayal. Love is a lie. Love is manipulative.
Love is cheap. At least, that's what you showed me,
and unfortunately, I believed you. I believed you for
a long time. But I don't want to believe you anymore.
Who gave you the power to decide the "kind of" love
I was worth anyways? The truth is-- I did. It's not an
easy pill to swallow. Maybe I didn't know any better.
Maybe I ignored the red flags. Either way, that power is
no longer yours. This is where you end, and I begin.

Dear reader,

I am complete. I pray seeds were planted between the lines, between the parallels of our hearts. I pray the spark that ignited these words in my heart, would fan into flames in yours; that those flames would bring light to help guide the way home. Darkness is simply the absence of light. If we have given up on finding love within others, it is only because we have given up on finding it within ourselves.

Sending love,
Levi